# THE WORLD AROUND YOU

# MEASURING AT HOME

by
Christianne Jones

PEBBLE
a capstone imprint

Published by Pebble, an imprint of Capstone
1710 Roe Crest Drive, North Mankato, Minnesota 56003
capstonepub.com

**Library of Congress Cataloging-in-Publication Data**
Names: Jones, Christianne C., author.
Title: Measuring at home / by Christianne Jones.
Description: North Mankato, Minnesota : Pebble, [2022] | Series: The world around you | Audience: Ages 5-8 | Audience: Grades K-1 | Summary: "Your house is packed with big things and small things and everything in-between. How tall is your refrigerator? How long is your bed? How wide is your door? Colorful photographs and interactive, rhyming text will have early learners ready to measure after reading this picture book"-- Provided by publisher.
Identifiers: LCCN 2021043785 (print) | LCCN 2021043786 (ebook) | ISBN 9781663976475 (hardcover) | ISBN 9781666326598 (paperback) | ISBN 9781666326604 (pdf) | ISBN 9781666326628 (kindle edition)
Subjects: LCSH: Measurement--Juvenile literature.
Classification: LCC QA465 .J66 2022 (print) | LCC QA465 (ebook) | DDC 530.8--dc23/eng/20211014
LC record available at https://lccn.loc.gov/2021043785
LC ebook record available at https://lccn.loc.gov/2021043786

**Editorial Credits**
Editor: Christianne Jones; Designer: Brann Garvey; Media Researcher: Svetlana Zhurkin; Production Specialist: Laura Manthe

**Image Credits**
Getty Images: RyanJLane, cover (top); Shutterstock: Alexia Khruscheva, 29 and 31 (top left), Andrei Zveaghintev, 19, ART_Photo_DN, 11, Bilanol, 28 and 30 (top right), BondRocketImages, 8–9, DGLimages, 14, dotshock, 10, Eric Isselee, 29 and 31 (middle), fizkes, 24–25, 26, 27, Followtheflow, 20–21, Hit1912, 28 and 30 (bottom), hitryuliya, 28 and 30 (middle), Jaromir Chalabala, 18, Juice Dash, 16, Juliya Shangarey, 3, KK Tan, 15, Mallika Home Studio, 23, Monkey Business Images, 22, New Africa, 6–7, Photographee.eu, 12–13, Prostock-studio, 17, Ruslan Semichev, 28 and 30 (top left), ventdusud, 29 and 31 (top right), wavebreakmedia, cover (bottom), Werner Lerooy, 29 and 31 (bottom)

Special thanks to Sveta Zhurkin and Dan Nunn for their consulting work and help.

# MEASURE UP!

Some toys are big and some toys are small.

You can use lots of words to measure them all.

Your house is filled with tons of treasure,

so dig around and start to measure.

# MEASURE WITH WORDS

When rulers, tape measures, and scales aren't around, you can use measuring and comparing words to describe what you've found!

**SIZE**
BIG/SMALL

**LENGTH**
LONG/SHORT

**DISTANCE**
NEAR/FAR

**WIDTH**
WIDE/NARROW

**DEPTH**
DEEP/SHALLOW

**WEIGHT**
HEAVY/LIGHT

## CAPACITY
### FULL/EMPTY

## HEIGHT
### TALL/SHORT

## TIME
### HALF HOUR/HOUR

## TIME
### LESS/MORE

## SPEED
### FAST/SLOW

## VOLUME
### LOUD/QUIET

# SIZE

A **BIG** dog and a **SMALL** cat are an unlikely pair. They have a loving friendship that is quite rare.

The dog is **BIGGER** than the cat.

The cat is **SMALLER** than the dog.

# LENGTH

The living room is spacious, open, and bright. A **SHORT** table and a **LONG** couch fit just right.

The table is **SHORTER** than the couch.
The couch is **LONGER** than the table.

# DISTANCE

You sit **FAR** from the TV during family movie night.

Then you snuggle into bed
to read **NEAR** a good light.

The TV is **FARTHER** away than the light.
The light is **NEARER** than the TV.

# WIDTH

A **NARROW** keyboard finds its place on the **WIDE** desk in your home office space.

The keyboard is **NARROWER** than the desk.

The desk is **WIDER** than the keyboard.

# DEPTH

A **SHALLOW** sink is a place for basic hygiene.

A **DEEP** bathtub is where you get squeaky clean.

The sink is **SHALLOWER** than the bathtub.
The bathtub is **DEEPER** than the sink.

# WEIGHT

A **HEAVY** suitcase
is packed up tight.

A **LIGHT** stuffed bear is squeezed just right.

The suitcase is **HEAVIER** than the bear.
The bear is **LIGHTER** than the suitcase.

# CAPACITY

A hungry puppy holds an **EMPTY** dish.

The dog dish is **EMPTIER** than the fish aquarium.

An aquarium **FULL** of water is home to some fish.

The fish aquarium is **FULLER** than the dog dish.

# HEIGHT

The plants in the back are **TALLER** than the ones in front.

Plants give your home a colorful hue. **TALL** or **SHORT**—any plant will do!

The plants in front are **SHORTER** than the ones in back.

# TIME

It takes about **HALF AN HOUR** to prep and mix the cake batter.

Prepping and mixing takes **LESS** time than baking the cake.

It takes close to an **HOUR** for it to bake, then you let it cool on a platter.

Baking the cake takes **MORE** time than prepping and mixing the batter.

# SPEED

The big red car moves across the floor at a **FAST** pace. The little blue car is **SLOW** and will not win this race.

The red car is **FASTER** than the blue car.

The blue car is **SLOWER** than the red car.

# VOLUME

Spend some **QUIET** time drawing a fluffy cloud.

Sing your favorite song and be really **LOUD**!

Drawing is **QUIETER** than singing.
Singing is **LOUDER** than drawing.

# MEASURING QUIZ

**1.** Is the cup **full** or **empty**?

**2.** Is the black car **near** or **far**?

**3.** Is the turtle **slow** or **fast**?

**4.** Is the train **short** or **long**?

The answers are on page 30.

# COMPARING QUIZ

**1.** Which dog is **bigger**?

**2.** Which child is **shorter**?

**3.** Which animal is **heavier**?

**4.** Which vehicle is **louder**?

The answers are on page 31.

# MEASURING QUIZ ANSWERS

1. The cup is **full**.

2. The black car is **near**.

3. The turtle is **slow**.

4. The train is **long**.

# COMPARING QUIZ ANSWERS

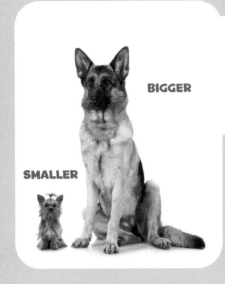

BIGGER

SMALLER

1. The dog on the right is **bigger**.

TALLER

SHORTER

2. The girl is **shorter** than the boy.

HEAVIER

LIGHTER

3. The elephant is **heavier** than the mouse.

LOUDER

QUIETER

4. The bus is **louder** than the bicycle.

# LOOK FOR THE OTHER BOOKS IN THE WORLD AROUND YOU SERIES!

  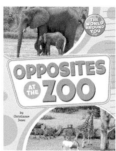  

## AUTHOR BIO

**Christianne Jones** has read about a bazillion books, written more than 70, and edited about 1,000. Christianne works as a book editor and lives in Mankato, Minnesota, with her husband and three daughters.